CLOSER LOOK AT
DESERTS AND WASTELANDS

Cally Oldershaw

COPPER BEECH BOOKS

Bro
ut

© Aladdin Books Ltd 1999
Designed and produced by
Aladdin Books Ltd
28 Percy Street
London W1P 0LD

*First published in the United States
in 2000 by*
Copper Beech Books, an imprint of
The Millbrook Press
2 Old New Milford Road
Brookfield, Connecticut 06804

Editor
Michael Flaherty

Designer
Jeff Gurney

Picture Research
Brooks Krikler Research

Front cover illustration
Gary Edgar-Hyde

Illustrators
Gary Edgar-Hyde, Mike Saunders, Peter Kesteven,
Stephen Sweet – Simon Girling and Associates,
Ian Moores, Rob Shone

Certain illustrations have appeared in
earlier books created by Aladdin Books.

Printed in Belgium

Library of Congress Cataloging-in-Publication Data
Oldershaw, Cally.
Deserts and wastelands / Cally Oldershaw.
p. cm. -- (Closer look at)
Summary: Explores different desert environments
around the world and describes the plants, animals,
and humans that live in them.
ISBN 0-7613-1152-1 (lib.bdg)
1.Desert ecology-Juvenile literature.[1.Deserts.
2.Desert ecology. 3.Ecology.] I.Title. II.Closer look at
(Brookfield, Conn.)

QH541.5.D4 O43 2000
577.54--dc21   99-045544

5 4 3 2 1

CONTENTS

4. Introduction
6. What Is a Desert?
8. Desert People
10. Desert Animals
12. Desert Plants
14. Desert Remains
16. Old World Deserts
18. Deserts of the Americas
20. Deserts of Australia
22. Frozen Deserts
24. Spreading Deserts
26. Desert Resources
28. Using the Deserts
30. Desert Facts
31. Glossary
32. Index

INTRODUCTION

Deserts cover more than a third of the land surface of the earth. They are found in every continent, from the frozen wastelands of the polar regions and the cold peaks of the Himalayas to the hot, arid Sahara Desert. With little or no water, deserts and wastelands seem desolate and empty places. But despite the extreme conditions, there is life in these regions. In order to survive, animals and plants have evolved some amazing features, such as the camel's hump and the cactus's spines and juicy stem. Deserts also contain materials useful to us, such as oil, gold, diamonds, and other minerals.

Fossil sand dunes

Captured in this sandstone (above) are the images of ancient sand dunes. Known as current bedding, this is typical of deserts and can be used by geologists to show how the rocks were formed.

Rusting sand

Desert sand is made mainly of the mineral quartz, but other minerals give the sand different colors. Sand that contains iron or other metals may rust in the air, creating red (below) or brown sands.

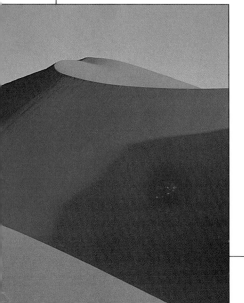

D eserts are not found randomly, bu follow zones around the world. Th size and shape of a desert does no stay the same, but may expand or shrink as the climate changes over hundreds or thousands of years. Deserts have less than 10 inches of precipitation (rain, snow, or dew) a year. When it does rain, it may be as a heavy storm that causes flooding.

WHAT IS A

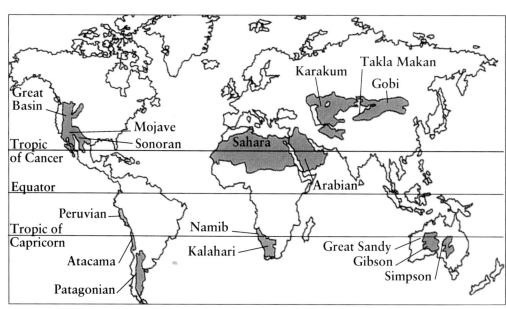

DESERT DISTRIBUTION

Deserts may be divided into different types, depending on where they are. At the poles are the freezing deserts of the Arctic and Antarctic. Next are the cold deserts of the tundra. The hot deserts lie along the Tropics of Cancer and Capricorn on either side of the equator (above). Local weather conditions can also cause deserts in other places, such as alpine (mountain) deserts, coastal deserts, and rain-shadow deserts.

The desert wind, carrying grains of sand, carves spectacular desert scenery. The sand grains are too heavy to be carried far by the wind. They bounce along, being lifted about 3 feet off the ground, and scour rocks into mushroom–shaped pedestals (right).

DESERT?

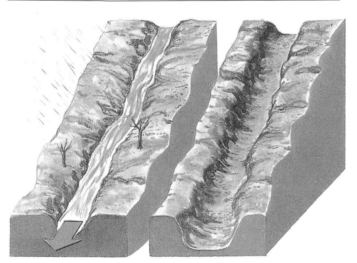

Rain-shadow deserts

Rain-shadow deserts are formed where mountains along the coast keep the rain from reaching further inland. The warm, moist wind blows toward the mountains, where it rises and cools to form clouds. Rain falls from clouds over the mountains. Beyond the mountains the air is too dry to rain, creating a rain shadow. Deserts such as the Great Basin, Sonoran, and the Patagonian deserts are formed in the rain shadow of the mountain ranges along the western margin of the Americas.

Clouds form and rain falls on the mountains.

WADI WATERS

The rare but heavy desert storms cause sudden "flash" floods — there is so much water that the ground cannot soak it all up. The water carries lots of sand and soil, cutting a deep groove, called a wadi, into the landscape (above). When the waters disappear, these river channels are left behind. Each storm makes the channels wider and deeper.

Warm, moist air rises and cools.

Dry air warms as it sinks.

Many desert dwellers wear loose-fitting clothes and cover their heads and faces to protect themselves from the sun, the heat, and the cold desert nights. The dark skin of such people as the Australian Aborigines and the bushmen of the Kalahari acts to prevent their skin from burning under the harsh sun.

On the road

The Bedouin (above) are desert people of northern Africa and Arabia. Bedouin means "desert dweller" in Arabic. Many have now settled in villages. Others continue the traditional nomadic life. They live in tents, raise horses and camels, and train peregrine falcons to hunt hares and birds.

DESERT

The blue men

The Tuareg are nomadic people of the Sahara. The Tuareg men wear distinctive dark blue clothing and cover their faces (below). They are known as the "blue men" because the dye rubs off on their skin from their clothes.

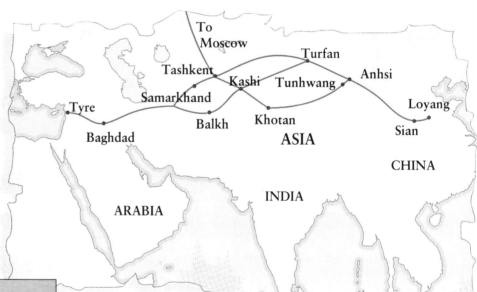

To Moscow
Turfan
Tashkent
Kashi
Tunhwang
Anhsi
Samarkhand
Tyre
Khotan
Loyang
Balkh
Sian
Baghdad
ASIA
CHINA
INDIA
ARABIA

THE SILK ROAD

The Silk Road is the ancient overland route by which traders once brought silk and spices from China and the East to trade for goods, silver, and gold from the Roman Empire and the West (above). The 4,340-mile route runs through the mountains and deserts of Asia, skirting both the Gobi and the Takla Makan deserts (see map on page 6).

ON CLOSER INSPECTION
— *Frankincense*

Frankincense is the hardened resin that oozes from the bark (right) of *Boswellia* trees found in desert areas of East Africa and the Middle East. It is burned as incense and gives a spicy smell. It was given by the wise men to the baby Jesus in Bethlehem.

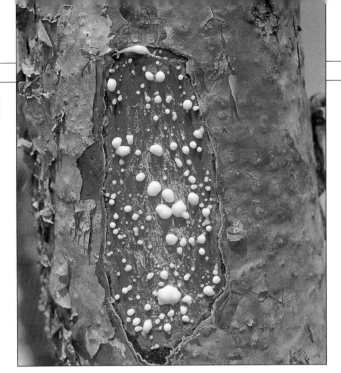

PEOPLE

NOMADS

Nowadays desert dwellers live mainly as traders and herders. Many have a nomadic life, moving their herds of camel, goat, or sheep from place to place looking for grazing (below) and carrying goods to trade. They take with them their tents and all their belongings, packed on the backs of camels or donkeys. Large groups of camels (camel caravans) loaded with trade goods still cross the Sahara of Africa and the Gobi of Asia.

Dwelling down under
The native people of Australia, the Aborigines (above), have learned to survive the hot, arid climate of the Australian "outback" — remote inland country. Traditionally, they have hunted for food by throwing spears and boomerangs at animals such as kangaroos. The hunting boomerang has a range of up to 295 feet in the hands of an expert. The Aborigines also learned how to find nutritious grubs in tree roots and water or moisture in plants.

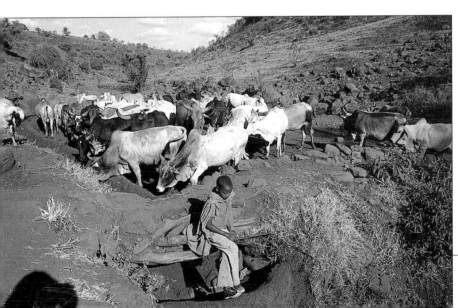

To survive in the desert, animals have adapted a number of ways to cope with the hot days, cold nights and the lack of water. Some use burrows or dig into the sand to avoid the heat of the day. Many are only active in the cooler parts of the day or at night. Others, such as fennec foxes and desert hedgehogs, have large ears to help lose excess heat.

DESERT

Sidewinders

Many poisonous animals, such as sidewinding snakes, make their home in hot deserts. Sidewinders move sideways over the hot sands (above), with only two points of their bodies touching the ground at any one time. This method of movement works well over shifting sand.

Stumpy

The stump-tailed skink (below) of Australia is a desert carnivore (meat eater). It is well suited to its desert surroundings. It conserves water by storing it as fat in its tail. Another lizard that does this is the Gila monster of the southwestern United States and Mexico.

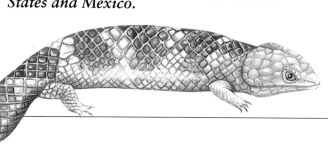

GETTING OUT OF THE HEAT

During the day, some mammals, like Arizona jackrabbits, find shelter in the shade of a cactus. Many others live in burrows and are only active at night. Their fur helps to keep them warm in the cold desert night. The temperature inside the burrow doesn't change as much as the temperature outside. The American kangaroo rat seals itself inside its burrow during the day. As it breathes out, its breath helps to keep the burrow moist, which helps stop the kangaroo rat from losing too much water.

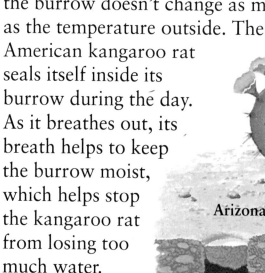

Arizona jackrabbit

Kangaroo rat

On Closer Inspection
— *One hump or two*

Camels can go for long periods without drinking. They survive by using fat stored in their humps. As the fat is used up, the humps shrink. A camel may have one hump (dromedary) or two humps (bactrian, right).

ANIMALS

LIVING ON A YUCCA

The yucca, or Joshua tree, is found in Mexico and the southwest United States. Desert animals use the plant as a home, as somewhere to hide, and as food. The yucca is eaten by herbivores (plant eaters), such as rabbits or tortoises. These, in turn, are eaten by carnivores (meat eaters), such as snakes. The cactus wren may nest in the yucca. The elf owl nests in holes made by woodpeckers. The weevil and the yucca moth depend upon the yucca for their food and the yucca depends upon the moth to pollinate its flowers. Termites feed on the dead branches, helping to break them down and return the nutrients to the soil, where worms, insects, and spiders live.

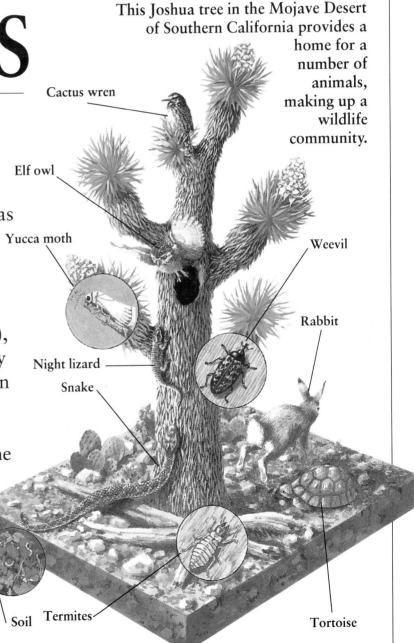

This Joshua tree in the Mojave Desert of Southern California provides a home for a number of animals, making up a wildlife community.

Cactus wren

Elf owl

Yucca moth

Weevil

Night lizard

Rabbit

Snake

Soil

Termites

Tortoise

To survive in the desert, many plant have ways of obtaining and saving what little water there is. Cacti and other desert plants are able to store large amounts of water in roots, stems, or leaves. Roots may grow deep or spread over a wide area. Because of the competition for water, such plants cannot grow very close together.

DESERT

Old World succulents

Many desert plants are succulents and store water in the fleshy tissues of their trunks, leaves, and branches. Succulent means "juicy." A thick, waxy coating protects the plants from water loss, even in the midday heat. Succulents can also close their stomata (pores) during the day to avoid losing moisture. They then open them in the cool of the evening or after a rainfall. Succulents are found on every continent. They include this aloe plant (above) of the Kalahari Desert in southern Africa.

SPIKY CACTUS OF THE NEW WORLD

The ridges on the stems of cacti, like this barrel cactus (left), allow the stems to swell, especially after heavy rainfall. The spikes are reduced leaves and help protect the plant from herbivores. The roots are shallow and spread widely around the cactus to absorb all available moisture. Some cacti are well known from cowboy movies. One such cactus, the saguaro (see page 19), is so popular as a garden plant that it is now protected by law in an effort to stop thefts.

On Closer Inspection
— *Islands of water*

In some parts of a desert, water from underground rocks may come to the surface. Plants grow up around such a spring. This is called an oasis (right). Desert animals and people rely on this water to survive.

PLANTS

This desert poppy completes its life cycle within a few days after a desert rainstorm.

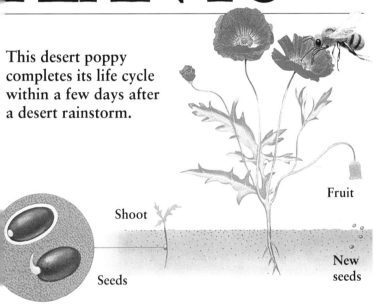

Seeds

Shoot

Fruit

New seeds

The desert in bloom

After a heavy rain, there is very little time for desert plants to grow, flower, and produce their seeds before the desert is again too dry. Desert flowers are usually large and brightly colored. The desert becomes a carpet of many colors for a few weeks (below). The rain also triggers the hatching of insects from their eggs. The insects are attracted to the brightly colored flowers and pollinate them as they hunt for food.

DORMANT SEEDS

Plants need water for their seeds to sprout and produce flowers. Rain may come only once every several years in the desert. The seeds of desert plants may lie dormant for years. Some appear to dry out completely, but then sprout after the rain; others have a tough coat or a protective chemical covering to stop them from sprouting until there is enough rain for them to flower.

Cave paintings
Cave paintings more than five thousand years old survive in the Sahara. They show that men hunted herds of grazing animals before the Sahara became a desert.

The dry conditions of deserts help preserve evidence of the past. Cav paintings made by ancient people give us a view back in time. Mummified bodies and artifacts found in the Atacama Desert, Chile, and in the pyramids of Egyp tell us about the people of those times. Mammoths from the permafrost of the northern tundra are so well preserved tha we even know what their last meals were.

DESERT

MUMMIFICATION

The ancient Egyptians believed that after death the body could only go on to the afterlife if it had not rotted. Mummification prevents the bodies from rotting. The brain, liver, intestines, and lungs were removed. The body was then packed in natron salt (sodium carbonate) to dry it out. It was padded with cloth, oiled, and wrapped in long strips of linen, like bandages. The mummies have survived for more than two thousand years, hidden in burial chambers within the pyramids in the desert.

For the wealthy, the most elaborate and complete process of mummification took seventy days.

On Closer Inspection — *Dead Sea scrolls*

A collection of scrolls were discovered sealed in jars in caves on the northwest desert shores of the Dead Sea in Jordan. They are made of papyrus, a type of paper made by the ancient Egyptians, and contain writings over 2,000 years old that are still readable.

REMAINS

MUMMIES IN THE ATACAMA

Hundreds of human remains have been found near the oasis town of San Pedro de Atacama in Chile. The bodies have been dried out by the intense heat of the desert sun (below). These prehistoric remains may be as much as seven thousand years old.

In the freezing desert conditions of the mountains of Chile and Peru, the mummified bodies of children were found. Their frozen remains may be a result of child sacrifice to Inca gods around 500 years ago.

Dinosaurs of the Gobi

Thousands of dinosaur fossils (above) have been found in the Gobi Desert of Asia, preserved in a landscape that gets only about 8 inches of rainfall a year. The first dinosaur expedition was led by the American Roy Chapman Andrews in 1922. He hit the news headlines when he found a group of dinosaur eggs arranged as if in a nest. Since then many fossils have been found, including complete skeletons. Arid conditions have also helped preserve fossils in the Karroo in South Africa.

Antelopes

The large mammals of the Old World deserts include antelopes such as the oryx, addax, and dorcas gazelle (below). They can travel long distances and survive without drinking, getting the moisture they need from the plants they eat and dew. All have suffered from overhunting. In 1972, the last known wild oryx was shot. They are now protected, having been returned to the wild from captivity.

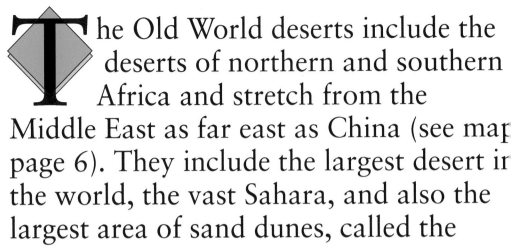

Dorcas gazelle

Addax

Oryx

T he Old World deserts include the deserts of northern and southern Africa and stretch from the Middle East as far east as China (see map page 6). They include the largest desert in the world, the vast Sahara, and also the largest area of sand dunes, called the Empty Quarter, in the Arabian Desert.

OLD WORLD

CHANGING SANDS

The wind blows sand into distinctively shaped piles or wavelike patterns called sand dunes. The shape and size of sand dunes depend upon the amount of sand and on the direction and strength of the wind (below). A gentle wind piles the sand into ridges, called transverse dunes, lying at right angles to the direction of the wind (1). A strong, steady wind blows the sand into long ridges, called longitudinal dunes, lying parallel to the wind (2). Barchan dunes are crescent shaped (3). They often form on rocky ground. Buffeted from all sides, star dunes (4) are quite stable, unlike barchan dunes, which may shift as much as 65 feet a year.

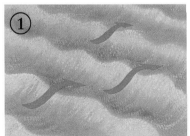

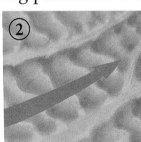

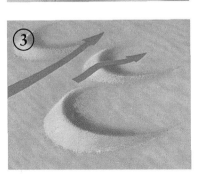

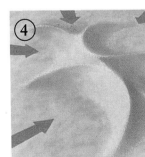

ON CLOSER INSPECTION — *Singing dunes*

The strange sounds of "singing" or "booming dunes" have been reported from deserts worldwide. The earliest reports are over twelve hundred years old from the Gobi Desert. The sounds are thought to result from the movement of sand.

DESERTS

THE MONGOLIANS

The Mongolians of Central Asia have traditionally been nomads, herding livestock for a living. They travel with their herds across the semiarid grasslands and the edges of the Gobi Desert. Mongolia gets its rain in a few summer storms. Today, many Mongolians live in permanent houses in the winter (below), but continue a nomadic life in the summer, living in traditional circular tents called gers or yurts. These collapsible structures have changed little since the Middle Ages.

BUSHMEN

The Bushmen of the Kalahari Desert in southern Africa are nomadic hunter-gatherers. They settle in an area where there is enough local game to hunt and vegetation to eat. Once supplies become scarce, they move on. The Bushmen use grass, leaves, and branches to make their homes (above). On a trek they may bury water-filled ostrich eggs to drink on the return journey.

Gypsum dunes
The white dunes in New Mexico (above) are made of gypsum crystals rather than sand. Gypsum is used to make plaster of Paris.

Colorado River
The Colorado River has cut a deep valley into the rock of the desert, clearly showing the different layers of rock laid down over millions of years.

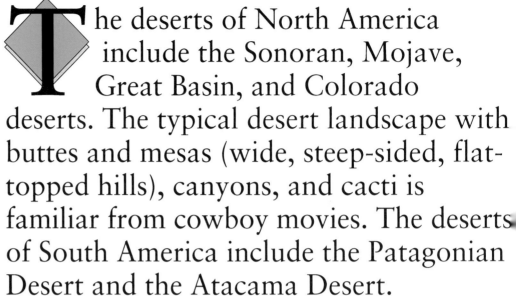

The deserts of North America include the Sonoran, Mojave, Great Basin, and Colorado deserts. The typical desert landscape with buttes and mesas (wide, steep-sided, flat-topped hills), canyons, and cacti is familiar from cowboy movies. The deserts of South America include the Patagonian Desert and the Atacama Desert.

DESERTS OF

DESERT LANDSCAPE
The strange-shaped rocks typical of the desert landscape of Colorado and Arizona are carved by wind and rain. Flash floods cut through hard surface rock, forming river channels or wadis, and ravines. Over thousands of years, rainstorms cut deeper and wider wadis, eventually isolating flat-topped, steep-sided hills called buttes from the larger mesas. Sand blown by the wind continues to wear away the softer rock, forming top-heavy structures called pedestals (see page 7).

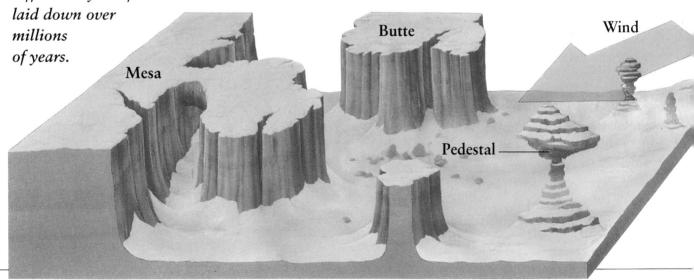

Mesa

Butte

Wind

Pedestal

Las Vegas and Palm Springs (right) are thriving desert towns. The inhabitants rely on modern technology to provide water and power. Without the constant supply of water pumped from the Colorado River, the towns would soon revert to desert.

THE AMERICAS

100—200 years (45 ft)

COASTAL DESERT

About 600 miles long, the Atacama Desert in Chile is bordered by the Andes to the east and the Pacific Ocean (above) to the west. It is a mineral-rich desert (see page 26) that receives less than half an inch of rain a year.

Saguaro cactus

There are about two hundred species of cactus. The largest cactus is the saguaro (right). It is found from southern Arizona to Mexico. The cactus grows slowly and can grow to more than 50 feet tall and live for more than two hundred years.

75 years

50 years

25 years

10 years

A ustralia's vast desert interior is mainly stony flatlands, scrublands and dunes. There are many plants and animals unique to Australasia, such as the kangaroo. Even so, the Australian hopping mice and Saharan jerboas look surprisingly similar, because they have each adapted to desert life by developing long hopping legs and a long tail.

Aboriginal artwork

Aborigines were living in Australia for at least fifty thousand years before the first Europeans arrived. Paintings (above), stories, and songs passed from generation to generation describe much folk knowledge, including routes across the interior, the positions of sacred caves, and sources of water and food.

The only survivor of the Burke and Wills expedition of 1861 was John King, who was found and rescued by Aborigines (below).

DESERTS OF

AUSTRALIAN EXPLORERS

By 1840 much of southeastern Australia had been explored and settled by Europeans. Charles Sturt headed inland but died in the Simpson Desert. Leichardt perished attempting the first east-west crossing of Australia in 1848. Eyre befriended the Aborigines and traveled with them. Burke and Wills ignored Aboriginal knowledge and tried to cross Australia from the south to the north coast. They encountered crocodiles and mosquitoes, and died in 1861 on their way back.

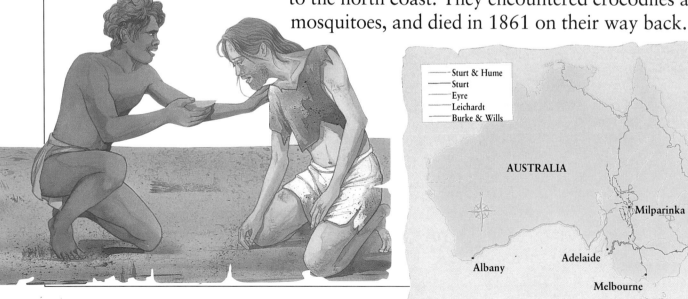

Sturt & Hume
Sturt
Eyre
Leichardt
Burke & Wills

AUSTRALIA

Milparinka   Brisbane

Adelaide   Sydney

Albany

Melbourne

ON CLOSER INSPECTION
— *Eucalyptus*

Many types of Eucalyptus are well adapted to the semiarid regions of Australia. Though not true desert plants, they survive the hot, dry conditions. Eucalyptus have oily leaves and some have white bark, both of which are protection against the sun's heat.

AUSTRALIA

KANGAROOS

Most of the native mammals of Australia are marsupials — the females have pouches in which they carry and nurture their young. The largest marsupial is the red kangaroo (left). An adult red kangaroo can be more than six feet tall. Kangaroos use their large hind legs to hop. This uses less energy than walking over the same distance. They can reach speeds of 31 miles per hour. Other marsupials include koalas, wombats, possums, and marsupial mice and moles.

Great Pebble
Rising 1,143 feet above the sandy Australian plain and almost 2 miles long, Uluru (meaning "great pebble"), formerly Ayers Rock, is one of the largest rocks in the world. It is a red sandstone mountain more than 450 million years old and is a sacred site of the Aborigines, who have decorated the rock's caves with paintings.

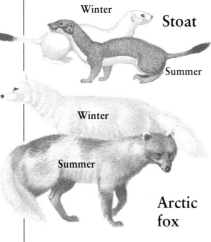

Winter

Stoat

Summer

Winter

Summer

Arctic fox

Tundra wildlife

On the marshy plains of the tundra, plants such as lichens, mosses, and sedges feed plant eaters, such as musk oxen, reindeer, arctic hares, and lemmings. These in turn are hunted by predators such as wolves, arctic foxes, and stoats. In winter, many of these animals grow white coats (above) to hide them in the snow.

The polar regions are frozen deserts. There is little or no rainfall, and the fresh water is usually held as ice and cannot be used by plants or animals. Over the North Pole is a vast cap of floating ice. The South Pole is an ice-covered landmass. Other frozen wastelands include the high-altitude deserts called alpine deserts.

FROZEN

LIFE ON THE FROZEN WASTES

There are few land animals in the polar regions. But the surrounding cold seas contain plenty of wildlife. In the Arctic, fish provide food for such animals as migratory sea birds, polar bears, and walruses, which live on the islands and ice floes (below). In the Antarctic, seals, penguins, and visiting sea birds also rely on food from the sea.

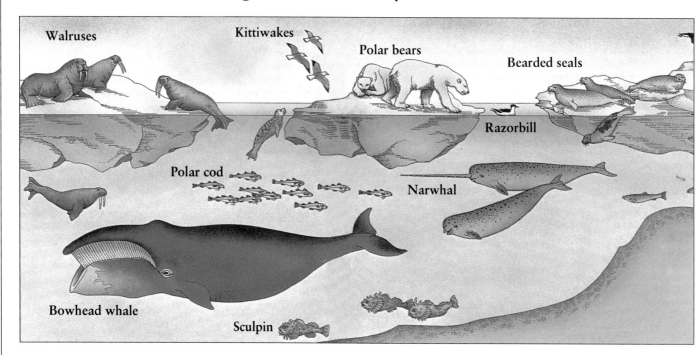

Walruses

Kittiwakes

Polar bears

Bearded seals

Razorbill

Polar cod

Narwhal

Bowhead whale

Sculpin

On Closer Inspection
— *Ice people*

Formerly known as Eskimos (raw fish eaters), about one hundred thousand Inuit (right) live in the Arctic desert. Some Inuit still hunt, more often using motorized sleds and motorboats than traditional kayaks (canoes) and dogsleds.

DESERTS

SCIENTISTS IN ANTARCTICA

Scientists study many aspects of the wildlife and the environment. Some study the composition of Antarctic waters, including pollutants that have reached them from populated areas of the world. Others analyze the chemicals found in snow and ice to determine an environmental history. Few scientists stay all year; most only visit for a few months in the summer.

Pingos

In winter, the tundra is blanketed by snow and ice. In the summer months, snow and ice melt (thaw) to form boggy, waterlogged marshes, but the ground beneath remains frozen all year round (permafrost). Pingos

form when underground water freezes and expands, pushing up these circular hills, which may be as much as 230 feet high (above right). Rock fragments roll down the sides of the pingos, forming paving stone-like patterns.

Polar plants

Many polar flowering plants have a slow life cycle. The seeds of scurvy grass on Spitsbergen in the Barents Sea take four years to ripen. The most common plants are mosses (below), lichens, and algae. Lichens grow very slowly — only about 2 inches every hundred years. Antarctica is home to only two flowering plants, a grass and an herb that survive summer temperatures just above freezing.

Over geological time, continents have moved and climates have changed. For example, 250 years ago New York was a desert near the equator. Deserts may also occur as a direct result of human activity over relatively short periods of time. Such activities as farming, grazing livestock, and tree felling may leave the land like a desert.

SPREADING

Famine
Many farming families living near desert areas, such as in parts of Africa, produce little more than they need to feed their own families. When there is a drought, the crops fail. Without food there is famine (above). Many people are forced to rely on charities and famine relief centers for food and medicine to survive.

OVERGRAZING
Scientists have calculated that in some places the Sahara has been spreading southward by as much as 31 miles a year. Some areas now covered by desert were rich farming areas just forty years ago. During the 1960s there was plenty of rainfall, and farmers increased the size of their cattle herds. But there were severe droughts during the next twenty years. The cows ate what little grass there was and many trees were felled for firewood. Without the grass and trees to hold the soil, the winds blew it away, leaving only desert.

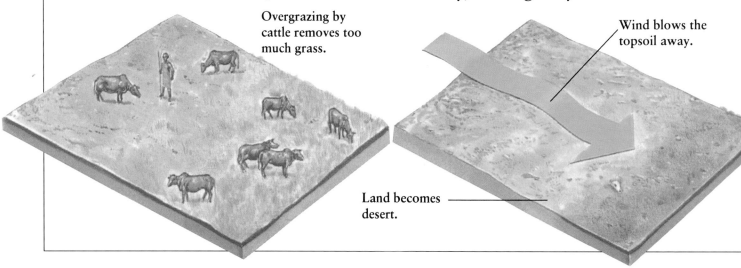

Overgrazing by cattle removes too much grass.

Wind blows the topsoil away.

Land becomes desert.

— *Grain for the Empire*

In about 30 B.C., Egypt became a province of Rome. The Romans introduced better farming methods, and Egyptian grain was used to feed Rome. Egypt became known as the grain bowl of the Roman Empire. Today, these areas have become desert.

DESERTS

CREEPING DESERTS

Wind blows sand into piles called dunes and may blow the dunes toward oases and settlements. In this way many crops and settlements have been covered by the creeping desert sands. By planting trees and grass, the roots help hold the sand in place, which slows the advance of the dunes.

Cotton fields

Cotton fiber (right) is picked, spun into thread, and used to make cloth. Since the 1920s, chemicals have been used to kill weeds and insects and also to increase the amount of cotton grown. But some of these chemicals are so poisonous they gradually destroy the soil so that it cannot support any crops. It becomes a desert.

Wind blows the sand along.

Sand advances over farmland.

Copper in Chile

Some of the largest mines in the world are the copper mines (above) in the Atacama Desert and high alpine deserts of the mountains in Chile. The highest mine in the world, at an altitude of 19,700 feet, is a sulfur mine, also in Chile.

The deserts are a source of great wealth. Gold, silver, diamonds, and other minerals are found in both hot and cold deserts. The Middle East has become prosperous through oil production, and oil in Texas and California has made many millionaires. In the Arctic Circle, oil and gas are transported in huge pipes, such as the trans-Alaska pipeline. The severe weather and the distances make exploration and extraction difficult.

DESERT

Gold rush

The Klondike in northwest Canada was the center of the gold rushes of the 1890s (above). More than 100,000 fortune seekers headed for the Klondike, but fewer than 30,000 survived the hardships of the journey.

PRETTY PEBBLES

In the deserts of southern Africa, diamonds are a valuable resource. They were formed at great temperatures and pressures deep underground. The diamonds are mined from rare volcanic rocks in which they form, called kimberlite (below). As the rock is worn away by the weather, the diamonds are released. They may travel great distances in rivers and may even reach the sea. Diamonds collected from the desert sands of the Namibian coastline and the coastal waters have been washed down from diamond-bearing rocks further inland.

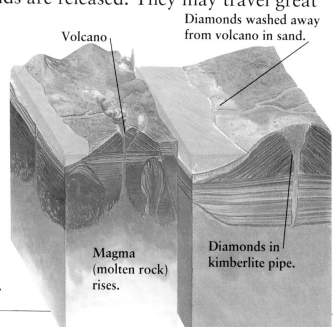

Volcano

Diamonds washed away from volcano in sand.

Magma (molten rock) rises.

Diamonds in kimberlite pipe.

ON CLOSER INSPECTION
— *An underground town*

Coober Pedy (right) is Australia's largest and oldest opal mining town, with a population of over 2,000. The desert conditions have driven the population underground, not only to mine, but also to live. The houses are built with only part of the house and the roof above ground.

RESOURCES

Southern bounty

Geologists have found evidence of coal and metal ore deposits in Antarctica (below) and possible oil deposits offshore. In order to protect the environment and to keep Antarctica as a wilderness park, mining and most forms of development in Antarctica are banned by the international Antarctic Treaty.

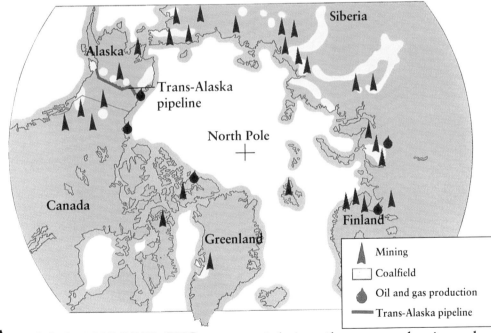

Siberia

Alaska

Trans-Alaska pipeline

North Pole

Canada

Greenland

Finland

Mining
Coalfield
Oil and gas production
Trans-Alaska pipeline

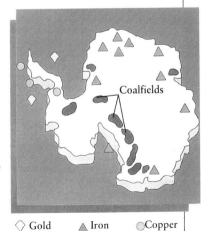

Coalfields

◇ Gold ▲ Iron ◎ Copper

ARCTIC RESOURCES

Traditionally, furs, caribou, and fish were resources of the Arctic. Today, attention is centered on vast coalfields that span the Arctic. The Arctic is rich in oil, gas, and minerals, but the extreme cold makes exploration difficult. Recently, diamonds were discovered in the tundra of the Northwest Territories of Canada.

Radio

Radio telescopes detect invisible radio waves from space. The focusing dishes need to be large, and deserts provide the space needed to build them (above).

Solar power

Solar power plants (below) are used to generate electricity from the sun's rays. The best place to build such plants is in deserts — the skies are clear all year round, allowing the strong rays to be collected.

The clear skies above deserts make them ideal for observatories. Deserts have also been used to tes nuclear bombs and to dump toxic waste. As deserts become more easily accessible, off-road sports such as "dune-busting" are becoming more popular, while nature reserves attempt to give some protection to the fragile desert wildlife.

USING THE

MARTIAN TERRAIN

Desert vehicles were developed by NASA to be used on the moon and Mars. In 1971 a lunar rover that had been tested in the Californian desert was aboard Apollo 15. Astronauts drove the lunar rover more than 17 miles on the surface of the moon. Sojourner (below), the small rover of the Mars Pathfinder probe in 1997, was tested in U.S. deserts.

On Closer Inspection
— *Clear skies*

Astronomical telescopes are used for observing stars and planets. To see the light from space, they need clear skies and to be away from the lights of towns and cities. Deserts and mountain tops provide the best conditions for using such observatories (right).

DESERTS

Dune busting
The large, empty expanses of deserts are used by off-road drivers. Each year more than one hundred contestants take part in the Paris-to-Dakar car rally through the Sahara Desert, often off-road and using satellites to find their way. Specially designed "dune buggies" (below) are used in the sport of "dune busting," a particularly popular sport in the Mojave Desert, California.

NUCLEAR TESTING

Deserts worldwide have been convenient locations for nuclear testing and waste disposal, including toxic waste. In 1945, the world's first atomic bomb test took place in New Mexico's White Sands region. Since then, hundreds of atomic bombs have been detonated at test sites in deserts around the world. Since 1963, only underground nuclear testing (above) has been allowed in the United States.

The strongest image you have when you think of a desert is probably a sea of sand dunes, but most deserts consist of bare rocks and gravel, like this view of the Atacama Desert, Chile (above).

Antarctica's "dry valleys" are among the driest places in the world. They were carved by glaciers, which have now retreated, leaving the valleys ice-free. But life does exist here. Bacteria exist within the porous rock of these dry valleys, waiting for rare occasions when melted snow provides them with the water needed for life.

Death Valley in California is one of the hottest places on earth, with summer temperatures over 120.2°F.

Yuma, in Arizona is on record as the sunniest place on earth. Out of a possible 4,456 hours of sunshine a year, Yuma receives an average of 4,055 hours.

DESERT FACTS

The Sahara in northern Africa is the world's largest desert, covering 3,500,000 sq miles.

A dromedary camel can survive as long as ten days without water, living off fat in its hump. It can drink up to 106 quarts of water at one time.

The drought-resistant eggs of desert shrimps can survive up to 25 years waiting for rain. When the rains come, they have a short life. They must hatch, become adults, and lay eggs within a couple of weeks before the water dries up.

Age and the harsh climate of the Namib Desert cause the two leaves of the welwitschia plant to split into long shredded ribbons.

Young emperor penguins are cared for by their parent for six months.

Female emperor penguins lay a single egg on the Antarctic ice in the autumn before returning to the sea. The male rolls the egg onto his feet and covers it with his fat lower belly. Large groups of males huddle together like this to keep warm for two months without food or water in temperatures of -58°F. Even so, the eggs are kept at a temperature of 91.4°F.

In the Namib Desert of Africa grows a bizarre–looking dwarf tree called welwitschia. I has a huge taproot over 5 feet wide and only two leathery, green leaves that continue to grow all the plant's life. Slow-growing, welwitschia lives between one thousand and two thousand years.

The highest temperature recorded in the shade was 136.4°F at Al'Azizyah, Libya, in 1922.

Aborigine The native people of Australia, who lived in Australia thousands of years before it was discovered by Europeans.

Altitude The height of the land above sea-level.

Bedouin A nomadic people of the Arabian Peninsula and northern Africa.

Desert An area that has little or no rain, generally accepted to have a rainfall of less than 10 inches a year.

Dune Sand piled up by the wind into a hill or ridge.

Erosion The removal of rock or soil by wind or water.

Flash flood Flood caused by a sudden heavy rainstorm on land in an area that is usually dry.

Germinate The first stage in the growth and development of a seed into a new plant.

Irrigation Redirecting water by damming or moving water in pipes or channels to water crops in an otherwise dry area.

Mammal Warm-blooded animals that feed their young with their own milk.

Mummy Human or animal remains that have been preserved by drying out or freezing. Ancient Egyptian mummies were treated with oils and then wrapped in strips of linen, like bandages.

Nocturnal animals Animals that are active during the night and rest during the day.

Nomads People who have a wandering lifestyle, moving from place to place rather than settling in one place.

Oasis A place in a desert where water is near enough to the surface for trees or other vegetation to grow.

Outback The arid and semiarid areas in the interior of the continent of Australia.

Papyrus A paperlike material made from the stems of the papyrus plant.

Permafrost A layer of ground that is permanently frozen, above which a thin surface layer melts during the summer.

GLOSSARY

Pingo A circular hill pushed up as water below ground freezes.

Rain-shadow desert A desert formed beyond a mountain. It doesn't rain because the warm air has already dropped its water on the other side of the mountain or on the mountain as it passed over it.

Tuareg Nomadic people of the Sahara Desert.

Tundra A band of land in the Northern Hemisphere, stretching from North America to Russia and Eurasia, that borders the Arctic Circle. There are few trees and the ground is covered with snow for more than half the year.

Wadi A steep-sided valley formed by flash flooding in dry regions during a heavy rainstorm.

Weathering The process by which rocks are broken down by rain, wind, and frost (the weather).

INDEX

Aborigines 8, 9, 20, 21, 31
air 7, 31
aloe 12
altitude 22, 31
Antarctic 6, 22, 23, 27, 30
Arctic 6, 22, 23, 26, 27, 31
artifacts 14

bedouin 8, 31
Bushmen 8, 17
buttes 18

cactus 4, 10, 11, 12, 18, 19
camels 4, 8, 9, 11, 30
canyons 18
caravans 9
carnivores 10, 11
caves 14, 15, 20, 21
chemicals 23, 25
climate 6, 9, 24, 30
crocodiles 20

deserts:
  Atacama 14, 18, 19, 26, 30
  Australian 20
  Colorado 18, 19
  Gobi 8, 9, 15, 17
  Great Basin 7
  Kalahari 8, 12, 17
  Patagonian 7, 18
  Sahara 4, 9, 14, 16, 24, 29, 30, 31
dinosaurs 15
dunes 16, 17, 18, 20, 25, 28, 29, 30, 31

equator 6, 24
erosion 24, 31

famine 24
flash floods 7, 31
flowers 11, 13, 23
food 13, 17, 20, 22, 24, 30
fossils 6, 15

geologists 6
germinate 31
Gila monster 10
gods and goddesses 15
gold 4, 26, 27
grasses 17, 23, 24, 25
gypsum 18

herders 9
horses 8
hunting 8, 9, 13, 14, 17, 22, 23

ice 22, 23, 30
insects 11, 13, 25
irrigation 31

Joshua trees 11

kangaroos 9, 20, 21

leaves 12, 17, 21, 30
lichens 23

mammals 10, 16, 21, 31
mesas 18
minerals 4, 6, 19, 26, 27
mines 26, 27
mosses 23
mountains 6, 7, 8, 19, 21, 26, 31
mummies 14, 15, 31

nocturnal animals 10, 31

nomads 8, 9, 17, 31
nuclear bombs 28, 29
nutrients 11

oases 13, 19, 25, 31
oceans and seas 19, 22, 26, 30
oil and gas 4, 26, 27
outback 9, 31

papyrus 15, 31
permafrost 14, 23, 31
pingos 23, 31
plants and vegetation 9, 11, 13, 16, 17, 21, 22, 23, 30, 31
poles 6, 22, 23, 27
pollutants 23
power 19, 28
precipitation 6
predators 22

quartz 6

rain 7, 12, 13, 15, 17, 18, 19, 22, 24, 30, 31
rain-shadow deserts 6, 7, 31
rivers 7, 18, 19
rocks 7, 13, 16, 18, 21, 26, 30, 31
roots 12, 25
rust 6

sands 6, 7, 10, 16, 17, 18, 25, 30, 31
sandstone 6, 21
seeds 13, 23, 31
shoots 13
Silk Road 8
skeletons 15
skinks 10
snakes 10, 11
soils 7, 11, 24, 25, 31
spices 8
spiders 11
stems 12
stomata 12

storms 6, 7, 17, 18, 31
sun 8, 21, 28, 30

telescopes 28, 29
temperature 10, 23, 26, 30
tents 8, 17
termites 11
traders 8, 9
trees 9, 11, 21, 24, 25, 30, 31
tropics 6
  Cancer 6
  Capricorn 6
Tuareg 8, 31
tundra 6, 14, 23, 27, 31

wadi 7, 18, 31
water 4, 7, 9, 10, 12, 13, 19, 20, 22, 23, 26, 30, 31
weather 6, 26, 30, 31
weathering 31
whales 22
winds 7, 16, 18, 24, 25, 31

Photo Credits
Abbreviations: t–top, m–middle, b–bottom, r–right, l–left.
Pages 1, 2-3, 5, 6t, 8, 9t & m, 14 all, 17t & m, 18m, 20, 23m, 24, 25, 26t, 27, 28t, 29t & m — Frank Spooner Pictures; 6t & 23t — Bruce Coleman Collection; 9b, 13b & 23b — Hutchison Library; 13t, 19m & 30 — Cally Hall; 17b — Susanna van Rose; 18t — Roger Vlitos; 19t — Robert Harding Picture Library; 21t — Spectrum Colour Library; 21b — Emma Wild; 26b — Corbis/Bettmann; 28br — Sandia; 29b — Rex Features.